The Keeper of Stories and Joys

By

Bobbie J. Lane

DEDICATION

This book is dedicated to my grandmother Bonnie, who tirelessly made up bedtime stories to help me sleep as a child...and to my own children and grandchildren.

Bobbie Lane

ABOUT THE AUTHOR

Bobbie Lane resides in Texas and is currently pursuing a Bachelor's degree in Criminal Justice through Colorado Technical University. She is the proud mother of five grown children, a grandmother of nine, and a great-grandmother of one. Recently widowed, Bobbie has returned to her passion for writing, finding the time to bring her stories to life after many years.

Table of Contents

THE MAGIC HOLLOW

Introduction

Ari, who was ten years old, and her younger brother, Niko, were filled with excitement as they arrived at their grandparents' cottage for their spring vacation. Their grandparents, Bram and Mira, welcomed them with warm hugs and knowing smiles. The surrounding area, known as the Hollow, was a magical realm where Ari and 6-year-old Niko spent countless hours playing and exploring. The Hollow, with its ancient trees and hidden secrets, was a place where the ordinary world seemed to fade away, and the extraordinary came to life.

Once they arrived at the cottage, Grandma Mira fed them a snack. They ate as quickly as they could, anxious to go to their favorite playground.

When Children and Fairies Meet

Ari and Niko went outside and began playing the games they loved. They were playing hide and seek near the clearing in the Hollow when Ari noticed that the Hollow just beyond the clearing had a mystical calling about it, as if it were waiting for the children anxiously to embrace them with its magic.

Unknown to the children, 4 fairies named Lilibelle, Elira, Thistle, and Finn were just inside the Hollow on the fairy side. The veil between fairyland and humankind was thinning, so the fairies could easily see the children playing just within the Hollow on the human side.

As Ari and Niko wandered deeper into the Hollow, sunlight filtered through the canopy, painting the moss with dappled gold. The air shimmered with possibility, and a hush fell over the glade as if every living thing was poised for something extraordinary.

From the arch of trailing vines, Lilibelle peeked out, her wings fluttering with anticipation. Thistle, ever adventurous, perched on a low branch, while Finn hovered with an anxious smile, hoping the children would prove as gentle as they seemed. Elira, luminous and calm, drifted close behind, her presence like the soft touch of dawn.

But it was Pippa, the guardian of small joys and smaller feet, who kept a watchful eye on

Niko. She circled above his tousled hair, invisible yet close enough that he felt a tickle of laughter on his cheek and smelled clover, sweet and fresh. Pippa had always believed in the courage tucked inside little hearts and saw something in Niko that made her wings shimmer with pride.

The fairies whispered among themselves, deciding if it was finally time to reveal their presence. Ari paused, sensing a gentle tingling, as if the air around her was charged with secrets. She knelt beside a patch of violets, urging Niko to do the same.

Suddenly, Lilibelle emerged in a swirl of petal-light, her voice bright as bells. "Welcome to the Hollow," she said, bowing in greeting. Thistle, Finn, and Elira joined her, each fairy radiating a unique hue—emerald, silver, and soft blue—casting a gentle glow in the morning shadows.

Niko's eyes widened as Pippa appeared before him, her laughter ringing out in the hush of the glen. "I've watched over you, little explorer," she said kindly. "You've come so far with your courage and your curiosity."

In that moment, the Hollow brimmed with wonder and warmth. Secrets long held and stories half-told fluttered from branch to branch as fairies and children shared their first smiles and words. Ari and Niko listened, entranced, as the fairies spoke of the heartstone and the old magic of wishes. And so, with their meeting, the promise of adventure blossomed like a thousand wildflowers, eager to be discovered.

Ari and Niko spent most of the day with their new friends. Just as it was beginning to get dusky, the fairies led the children along the path to their grandparents' cottage. Once inside the house, Grandma Mira and Grandpa Bram are glad to see their grandchildren make it home safely. They really had not been too worried about them, though, for they also knew about the Hollow and all of its magical charm. Niko was the first to start telling them of their experiences in the Hollow with the fairies. Ari was afraid they would think they were telling stories, but Mira and Bram just looked at one another with a knowing smile on their lips.

Scene: The Dreams

That night, as the cottage settled into silence and the stars blinked overhead, the Hollow stirred. Ari dreamed first. They stood in the clearing again, but it was different—larger, older. The trees hummed with light, and the glowing log had split open like a book, revealing swirling symbols and tiny flickering scenes. Pippa floated nearby, her wings trailing stardust. She said, "You've awakened something." "The Hollow remembers you."

Ari reached out, and then the symbols rearranged into a map— not of places, but of stories. One showed Mira as a child, chasing fireflies. Another showed Bram speaking with a fox with silver eyes. "You're part of its memory now," Pippa whispered, "and it's part of yours."

Niko's dream bloomed next. He flew—not walked—through the forest guided by moon fern lights. Lilibelle and Thistle raced beside him, laughing. At the end of the path was a tree with a door carved into its trunk. Inside, shelves of glowing jars pulsed gently. One jar had his name on it. Niko opened it, and out poured laughter, music, and the scent of cinnamon. "You're a keeper now," Pippa said, "of joy, of stories."

The children awakened early the next morning. When they walked into the kitchen, Grandma Mira was cooking breakfast, and Grandpa Bram was sitting at the table, smoking his pipe and reading a tattered, well-weathered book. The children excitedly shared their dreams with them.

Grandma Mira said the Hollow does that when it wants you to return. It reaches out with its magic into your dreams. Grandpa put the book away and agreed with Mira. Grandma said to eat their fill because the Hollow doesn't like hungry guests.

After eating, the children headed back to the Hollow to meet up with their new friends, the fairies. Lilibelle, Thistle, Elira, and Finn were waiting for them expectantly; all of them were ready to spend another day in the Hollow with the children. Today, they would share a little more with them about the dilemma of the thinning veil and the imbalance of magic, which seemed to be getting worse every day.

Serious Finn was the first to bring it up. After all the fairies had welcomed them to the Hollow, Finn told the children that the dilemma was worsening and they really needed all the help they could get to try and find the answers.

Ari and Niko looked at one another and then at Finn. "What can we do? We are only children." Finn answered that their natural curiosity, their innocence, and courage could combine with the 5 fairies' magic and be very powerful tools.

Lilibelle added that their grandparents' wisdom and knowledge, which they've gained over the years of living in the Hollow, would also give them even more powerful tools to combat the imbalance.

The fairies were so worried that it was hard to play that day. The children decided to go get their grandparents for help.

Meanwhile, Bram and Mira had been talking. They had noticed that the veil was thinning and something wasn't quite the same as it had been over the years. For five fairies to show themselves to the children meant they were concerned for the well-being of fairyland in the

Hollow. They had already decided to share with the children their concerns and offer to help in any way they could.

Niko's dream of the Archive tree had given Grandfather a bright idea. They would all go to the Tree and see what memory would be there to guide them. Just as they were leaving to gather the children, they saw Ari and Niko scrambling their way. "Grandma, Grandpa!" "Can you please come help the fairies? The Hollow has an imbalance, and we hope that all of us together will be able to bring the balance back."

Their grandparents were glad to see them and headed out with them to the glen where the fairies spent most of their time among the beautiful flowers. The fairies even slept in the flowers at night. It wasn't far from the edge of the Hollow, and they soon joined with the fairies and told them their plan.

The fairies were so excited; even Finn couldn't hide his enthusiasm. Thistle fluttered his wings excitedly, and they all headed out to the Archive Tree. Of course, Pippa was there watching over Niko, especially. He was her boy now. Lilibelle and Elira were hesitant at first because they did not know the way and were used to leading the crew of fairies and watching over the humans. Soon enough, though, they had accepted the fact that Grandma and Grandpa had the best idea so far.

THE ARCHIVE TREE

Grandpa Bram pulled out a map he hadn't looked at in some time until earlier that morning to ensure that they didn't lose their way. It had been so long since they had been to the Archive tree. It had probably been 10 years or more. Ari hadn't even been born yet when they last visited.

It was like coming home in a way. They once spent so much of their time in the glen and the Hollow, exploring the glowing paths in the dappled sunlight. As Grandpa pulled the map out now, the whole map seemed to come alive again as it had once been. The paths on the map that led to the Archive Tree were lit up, and this made it so easy to follow.

As they walked, Grandma and Grandpa explained that the Archive Tree is a majestic and ancient tree within the Hollow, holding the collective memories of everyone who has ever been touched by its magic. Inside the tree, shelves of glowing jars pulse gently, each containing a unique memory. These jars are not just containers of memories, though; they are actually imbued with the essence of the Hollow's magic, responding to emotion and memory. When someone approaches the tree, it senses their emotional state and the specific needs of the moment. It chooses the memory that is most relevant to the current situation, offering guidance and insight. This selection process is not random. It is guided by the tree's deep connection to the Hollow's Magic and its understanding of the individual's past and present.

As Mira and Bram led the group to the Archive Tree, Niko ran ahead because he recognized the tree from his dream the previous night. He looked on the shelf and saw a jar with his name on it. He opened it, and laughter and kindness poured out, along with the smell of cinnamon and cloves. Pippa was hovering just above him and laughed along with Niko.

Mira and Bram reached on the shelf and took down a jar with Mira's name on it. Together, they opened it, and a scene unfolded, revealing Mira as a child guided by Pippa the fairy through a maze of glowing paths. The Hollow responds to emotion and memory, and the wonder and curiosity of a child is the key to restoring balance.

Grandma Mira was teary-eyed as she saw this memory and recalled how free she had felt at the time and how close she and Pippa had once been.

Before leaving, the fairies checked deep in the tree for any clues that may have been missed. They found a map with magical symbols and glowing paths to follow, much like Grandpa's map. Grandpa was able to decipher the symbols by comparing the maps to one another. He looked up at the group and said, "I know just where we need to go now!" "We need to see the Guardian. "

HAH
LAAHHHAH
Niko
Pippa

THE GUARDIAN

Grandma was not surprised by Bram's exclamation. She had experiences in the past that required a trip to the Guardian. She took Bram's hand and said, "It's time for lunch before we head that way."

The fairies sought out the perfect place for a picnic lunch. Grandma had a checkered tablecloth that she spread out over the ground. All around this area of the glen were flowers of all colors. Roses, yellow and red, bluebells, and sunflowers were abundant. The air here smelled so beautiful!

Grandma and Grandpa began unpacking the lunch, and Ari helped. Niko was so full of energy right now that he couldn't sit still. He played chase with the fairies, with Pippa giving him a little head start to make it more fun.

After eating the picnic lunch, Grandma leaned against a huge tree with a mischievous look in her eye. She made the comment that she once met the Guardian in this very place or one very much like it.

The children were excited to hear this and sat down to listen as Grandma and Grandpa explained. Once long ago, a similar imbalance had occurred. Mira and Bram were a part of the solution then. Grandma Mira said, "If we sit here for just a bit longer, perhaps the Guardian will make himself known to us. Even the fairies alighted from flight and sat very still and quiet for a few minutes. Niko had a hard time being still just now, so he was still running around playing among the flowers.

Suddenly, they became aware of a light breeze beginning to blow, and they all sensed a presence nearby that they hadn't noticed earlier. Even active little Niko realized that there was something different in the air and came to sit on Grandpa's lap.

Just then, they heard a voice saying, "Welcome to the Hollow." The voice sounded like bells ringing as if to awaken others from their reveries. The earth beneath them seemed to tremble a bit, just enough to get all the fairies and the children to listen as Grandma said, "Guardian of the Hollow, how wonderful to meet with you again." "Mira? Is that really you?" We haven't spoken in many years!"

Mira told the Guardian why they were here. She explained that the fairies had alerted them of an imbalance in the Hollow; she was here with Bram and the children to see how they could help the fairies in their quest to heal the land.

The Guardian said in a melodic voice that sounded like running water somehow, "They will need to gather the 4 Essences of Earth, Water, Wind, and Fire."

Once they had all of the essences, their next task would be much easier. Mira and Bram exchanged glances as they often did, and Mira asked the Guardian for some guidance on how to find the Essences. The wind picked up for a brief time, and they sensed that the Guardian had left them. Now, next to the picnic lunch was a book that had not been there before.

THE ANCIENT TEXT

Grandmother Mira picked up the book and handed it to Bram. He held it in his hand with reverence for the Guardian's gift. The cover of the book had ancient symbols on it, and inside the book were maps, stories, and directions to all of the important places that had been touched by the Hollow's magic.

According to the book, each Essence would be guarded by a creature. This would be a lot of traveling to get all of the essences of earth, wind, fire, and water. They needed to recoup and rest before venturing out. They needed to prepare for the journey, so they all headed home to the cottage. The fairies decided to stay in Grandma's flower garden for the night. Ari and Niko wanted to sleep outside with them, so Grandpa set up a small tent, and Grandma aired out the sleeping bags.

Throughout the night, the fairies and the children whispered to one another about the coming adventures and their plans. They even planned a surprise for Grandma Mira and Grandpa Bram. It would be their anniversary in about 2 weeks. That should be long enough for Ari and Niko to learn to bake a cake. Ari already knew the basics. The hard part will be getting all the ingredients together for the anniversary cake without Grandma knowing what was up. The fairies assured them that they could come up with all the ingredients, and Mira and Bram would never be the wiser.

They finally all slept until around 2 am until the light came into the garden at sunrise around 6 am. The children wanted to sleep a little longer, but they could hear Mira and Bram talking in the kitchen already and knew it would soon be time for breakfast.

They saw Grandpa Bram reading the ancient text to Grandma through the window and knew that it would be a day of big adventures. They kind of wished they had slept a little more, but were happy with the anniversary plans they had made.

It wasn't long before Grandma rang the cowbell and hollered that breakfast was on the table. The children and their fairy friends all came in to eat. Grandpa had finished eating already and began reading snippets of the ancient text to their fairy guests. He figured some of them might know what was being referred to as far as the magic needed to gain access to the 4 essences. Pippa listened very intently, as did Lilibelle and Thistle. Finn sat on Grandpa's shoulder in order to see the ancient runes and symbols. He was the scholar of the fairies and was very helpful. As for Elira, she was busy perusing Grandma's cookbooks for a wonderful anniversary cake that would hit the spot and be perfect for a golden anniversary!

Grandma Mira was very busy bustling around the kitchen to have baked goods to take on their journey. She also made some hushpuppies because they last a long time on the road. She made granola bars, which she hoped the fairies would love. She was frying chicken and baking pies, and the aromas were wonderful. The fairies soon were flitting about, trying to help her, but being a nuisance instead. Mira opened the door to the garden and shooed all the fairies out except for Finn, who was still helping decipher the ancient text.

Grandpa told the children to go and join their fairy friends outside while he and Finn concentrated hard on their task and doubled down on how much they were solving.

Grandma asked how long before they were ready to go out to the Hollow. Grandpa and Finn were so deep in thought that it took a few moments for them to answer her. It was determined that it would be best to stay home for one more night. There was still so much to be deciphered.

Grandma just said she would use the extra time to make extra food! Grandpa gave her a quick hug and thanked her for her understanding ways.

IN SEARCH OF THE ESSENCE OF THE EARTH

The next morning, they all had breakfast, and then Finn gathered the other fairies from the garden and told them all he could remember that he and Grandpa had deciphered from the ancient text.

Apparently, the first Essence we should collect is the Essence of Earth. The map has a maze of paths we must follow to find the guardian of the essence. "Come on, my fairy sisters and brother, let's get to it!" They were waiting near the edge of the clearing to the Hollow when the little family, all packed up and ready for the journey, came out of their house and headed their way.

"Good morning, everyone," Lilibelle exclaimed. "I am so ready to find this Essence of Earth." Elira and Thistle were eager to start the journey as well. Pippa was hovering over little Niko as she always did, as the keeper of small joys and smaller feet.

Thistle stayed close to Finn as Finn whispered all he could recall from the Ancient Text. Grandpa Bram headed up the group of little travelers with a confidence and happiness he had not felt in years. Grandma Mira saw the spring in his step and smiled a knowing smile. She didn't say it, but she knew he had needed a quest for some time. Having Ari and Niko were added bonus to the happiness and contentment she was feeling as well.

Lilibelle asked gently which way they were going. Finn said there were many paths on the map of the Ancient Text. Grandpa Bram said in his happy and booming baritone voice. "Just try to keep up. I know the way! Finn and I studied this all night long." The sun rose from the eastern horizon as they traveled forward with Bram leading the way. The fairies began singing a song, and the children joined in, and then Grandma. After several hours of traveling into the heart of the Hollow, Grandpa Bram stopped and said, "Here we are. "

The others looked around, hoping to see something extraordinary, but all they saw was more of the same—the same flowers, trees, and grasses they had been seeing. The rock formations even seemed too familiar, as if they were going in circles. But then, they saw it. There was a creature standing to the left of where they were in a shadow. It had the body of a large rabbit, kind of like the rabbit in the classic Winnie the Pooh tales, but this rabbit's fur was a deep green color, the same color as the forest. There were small flowers growing on his back. His eyes were a vivid blue and seemed to look right through you. He was extraordinary indeed. The Hollow's magic never disappoints. One never knows what they will catch sight of next. The creature spoke, "Good afternoon, travelers. What can I help you with? I sense the Guardian has sent you my way. Why?" The fairies began to speak in their soothing small voices, explaining to the rabbit creature that they were on a quest to restore balance to the Hollow. "The Guardian left an ancient text with directions for us." We had to do a lot of deciphering, but it has led us to you, kind sir." The creature smiled a little half-smile. I love to be a part of a good plan. I, too, have noticed the imbalance in the magical auras of the Hollow. I am so glad to see you and offer you what I am the guardian of.

Because of the wisdom and knowledge of your grandparents, the innocence and curiosity of the children, and the magic of your fairies, I will gladly give you the knowledge and ability to obtain Earth's Essence.

The tree that grows over my burrow gives me wonderful shade from the heat of the sun, but more than that, it holds the essence of the earth in its roots. To obtain it, you must all kneel by its roots and join your hands together, placing them palm down upon the roots.

The group did as they were instructed. As they knelt there, a glowing aura of light rose from its roots and floated into Grandpa Bram's outstretched arms. The light turned into a smooth stone, the color of ivory and turquoise. Bram admired the beauty of it lying in his aged hands. It seemed to radiate a warmth akin to a sunshiny day.

The creature, whose name was never mentioned, was nowhere to be seen. He had slipped into the Hollow's shadows.

The family of four and the five fairies felt that they were fortunate to have already gathered one of the four essences. For now, though, they needed to refresh and refurbish by eating some of Grandma's fried chicken and perhaps some apple pie. The fairies led the bunch to a glen of soft clover that was both shady and sunny at the same time, depending on which way the wind was blowing. The trees in this glen were likely older than Grandma and Grandpa's ages combined. There was a quiet reverence about the place. After eating, they all fell asleep and had some powerful, wonder-filled dreams in the Hollow.

DREAMSCAPES

All the fairies had curled up in flowers of the glen while the humans lay on the soft clover that made quite a nice bed. Grandpa and Grandma were snuggled together as they had been doing since the days of early courtship. They both had dreams of one another and secrets and magical scenes that both energized and relaxed them at the same time. It's as if the Hollow was rejuvenating them with these beautiful dreams of scenery and landscapes. The trees of the Hollow called to them as they slept. It was familiar to them both, having spent so many days living in the Hollow.

The children's dreams and the fairies' dreams were somehow combined and complemented one another. It's as if they were all in the same dream. They saw waterfalls cascading down cliffs and wind blowing through the trees, as evidenced by the leaves falling as in early autumn. They saw visions of Indian Summer, where the leaves were all different colors. There was both energy and peace in this shared dream. They all awakened at the same time, and somehow, without even speaking, they each knew what the others had dreamt.

They looked at Grandma Mira and Grandpa Bram still sleeping peacefully in one another's arms, their love and devotion to one another shining brightly and causing the children and the fairies to work on more plans for celebrating their 50th anniversary. They spoke in hushed whispers so as not to awaken their grandparents before they were ready. They all knew that their dreamscapes had been lovely. With all the wisdom of the ancient text in his knowledge now, Bram dreamt of the perfect path to the other essences. He and Grandma awakened shortly thereafter. They were in such harmony; they both knew the next mission would be to find the Essence of Water.

ESSENCE OF WATER

They all gathered their belongings and left the beautiful glen of clover and flowers. The aroma seemed to follow them, for the entire Hollow was in bloom. The children thought of how beautiful the Hollow would look in the snowy days of winter. They were both glad that, for now, there was no end to the warmth of the sun and the beauty of spring all around them. Grandpa Bram was once again leading the crew. His fairy helper, Finn, was hovering just above his shoulder so he could help guide them all to the right place.

They had walked for about 3 hours when they heard the rushing of water. They followed the sound and came upon a lively stream. It looked so refreshing. The children and Grandma Mira waded into the water barefoot and felt cool, slick stones beneath their feet. Grandpa Bram took this time to check the map they had been following. To him and Finn both, it looked like this was the place they needed to be to collect the Essence of Water. The cool stream seemed too calm to be making the sound of rushing water. They both compared the map to the watery landscape and discovered that there was a waterfall hidden beyond the canyon. They would have to be extremely careful if they were to locate the hidden waterfall. It may be too treacherous for humans, especially children.

Just as they were going to suggest that the fairies lead the way to the mysteriously hidden waterfall, the sound of rushing water changed somehow. The waterfall came into plain sight as if it were alive. From the midst of the Falls, a voice could be heard. This must be the guardian of the Essence of Water.

"Welcome," the voice said. "I have been expecting you."

Grandma and Grandpa could hardly believe their ears. The water was flowing freely and rapidly; yet this voice sounded as if it were coming from the very midst of the fall.

The fairies were entranced by the beauty of the cascading falls. Lilibelle and Elira flew a bit closer to get a better look at the mysterious Guardian of the Falls. If you looked at the Falls at an angle, you could clearly see a face in the water. "Hello, beautiful fairies," said the wet and slippery creature whose presence was like a rainbow. All the same hues that the fairies reflected with the fluttering of their wings. "Please come a little closer." I have what you are seeking; I guard what you are seeking. You are seeking the Essence of Water." "I know this because the Hollow has been speaking to me all morning about guests who are on their way to gather the necessary elements and heal the land of the imbalances it is experiencing. Come closer, dear fairy folk; you shan't be hurt." Pippa came forward, then Lilibelle, Thistle, and Fin. Elira was hesitant at first, but seeing the others go forward gave her the confidence to advance closer. The children and the grandparents also came closer. The creature said, "Reach into the waterfall with your right hand. Make a circle with your hands, and the element you seek will be yours." The group did as they were instructed, and lo and behold, a shard of light formed in the midst of the Fall, and Grandma was able to touch it and pull it close to her. When it was out of the water, the shard looked like a crystal rock with beautiful hues of red, yellow, and green. "There you are, my friends, and thank you for the wisdom and bravery you are all showing in your quest." "Soon, the Hollow will be back to its normal behaviors."

With the Essence of Water obtained, the family and the fairy folk headed back to the glen with the beautiful flowers. They needed to eat and rest to prepare themselves for the next leg of their journey. Lilibelle, Elira, Thistle, and Finn found flowers to sleep in. Pippa stayed close to Niko, protecting the little joys and smaller feet.

SLEEPING IN THE GLEN HALFWAY THROUGH THEIR QUEST

That night, the sky seemed clearer and larger than they had ever seen. It was as if the Hollow knew there would soon be a solution to its imbalance, and it was waiting for it expectantly. Grandma Mira spent a few hours cleaning their little camp and organizing their belongings. She wanted to be sure they could easily find anything they needed during the next leg of their journey.

The fairies were sleeping peacefully in the garden except for Pippa and Finn. She was ever watching over little Niko, as she always did. Grandma and Pippa had known one another since Mira had been a girl. Mira was so happy that Pippa was watching over her little grandson now. He was a brave little soul, sometimes venturing where he shouldn't. This sometimes worried Grandma Mira. Pippa was once again giving her peace of mind in her life.

Grandpa and Finn pored over the ancient text and maps they were following. They wanted to make the adventure as safe as possible. Thus far, the journey had been fairly uneventful; this worried Grandpa just a bit because life very rarely goes smoothly for very long at a time. As he and Finn deciphered more codes, Grandpa noticed that Grandma was a bit restless tonight. He called to her to come sit next to him. He held her hand as Grandma watched them work over the ancient text. Soon, she was calmer and lay down to rest.

During the night, Grandma had a dream. In her dream, she and her fellow travelers had obtained the Essence of Wind and Air in addition to the Essences of Earth and Water. In her dream, she knew the only Essence left was the Essence of Fire.

The four elements from which the essences come have always been on earth. Earth, wind, fire, and water dominate the processes of the world. Of the four essences, or elements, the essence of fire is the most dangerous and perilous. She woke from her dream feeling even more restless; she hoped this wasn't a prophetic dream of danger awaiting them.

Grandpa Bram and Finn had finally turned in. She lay next to Bram and could feel his strength next to her. She knew in her heart of hearts that this man was capable of so much protection. He had always and would always protect her and the children as well as their mystical companions, the fairies.

Mira reflected on all of the fairies' personalities for a while before falling back to sleep. There was Finn, the intellectual who was slow and steady of spirit…and Thistle, who loved adventures and thrived on adversity. Elira, the beautiful, and Lilibelle, the quiet and courageous spirit. She was happy and knew that the magic of the Hollow was at work, keeping the fairies from harm. The fairies had been an enchanted people for as long as Mira could remember, and long before she could possibly remember. As a child, Pippa had visited with her when her parents and her brothers and sisters had lived in their little cottage. She had met Bram when she was a child. They grew up with each other, and when the time was right, Bram had professed his love for her and asked for her hand in marriage. That was almost 50 years ago now. My, how time flies. Their marriage had been blessed from the beginning. She thought to herself, I must find something special to do for Bram for our anniversary this year. It was only two weeks away. It seemed fitting somehow that they were on this quest with their grandchildren. It reminded Mira of all the adventures she and Bram had experienced during their marriage at the beginning. There seemed to be no shortage of the amount of danger and feats of courage they had faced. One time stood out in her memory above all else….

THE FOX

Bram had gone hunting for meat in the Hollow. He preferred bringing home fresh meat for Mira rather than buying it at the market. On this particular day, he had been tracking a boar in the deep Hollow woods behind their cottage. Mira had been asleep when he left at the crack of dawn. He planned to get a boar if possible. They had venison already in their freezer. They could make some excellent sausage if he brought home a boar.

The depths of the Hollow were still dark, as the sunshine had not yet spread that deeply into the forest. The paths that were worn and well-traveled by Bram had come to an end as he was tracking the boar. Before he knew it, he had somehow turned around and didn't know which way to go. Continuing to track the boar hours later, Bram decided it was time to head home without the boar after all. The sun was high overhead now, and none of the familiar paths seemed to be in their usual place. It's as if the magic of the Hollow had somehow beguiled him into wandering too far and becoming lost. He knew Mira would be worried about him being out so late. He never wanted to give her reason to fret about anything in life. He had always been so protective and sensitive to her needs. Today was no different. He began looking for his own tracks into the Hollow and was slowly finding his way out when he saw a fox with silver eyes watching him. The fox would sit about 100 yards from him and wait for Bram to come closer before going further away from him. Once, after Bram had been backtracking for some time, the fox came up to him and sat and watched. Bram asked the fox his name. Surprisingly, the fox replied, "I am called Xanthe. I have come to help guide you out of the depths of the Hollow. Your hunt for a boar has beguiled you. Your love, Mira, is seeking you now." Just then, Xanthe let out a sound that almost sounded human, meant to alert Mira of their place in the Hollow. Xanthe had been watching Mira earlier in the day and heard her frantic cries for Bram. He had let her catch a glimpse of him as she was searching; his silver eyes had beckoned her, and she began following him out of instinct. As the fox led Bram from the depths of the Hollow, Mira was traveling toward Bram by virtue of the fox's trickery. It was as if the fox, Xanthe, had spun a web around her, keeping her on familiar paths while he helped Bram come home to her. Bram could hear Mira now, calling to him. He called back and thanked Xanthe for his help. The silver eyes held Bram's eyes in a long gaze. At that moment, Bram knew the Hollow had sent Xanthe to save the day. He could have been lost for days, but thanks to the wily fox, he could now hear Mira's voice and go to it.

As Grandma Mira thought back on this memory, she felt there was nothing their family and these beautiful fairy folk couldn't overcome in their desire to finish their mission of healing the imbalance. She finally drifted off to sleep and dreamed of Xanthe that night.

The next morning, they didn't get as early a start as they had wanted. When Finn and Bram opened the ancient text, there was a new symbol on the page, glowing in otherworldly light. Bram recognized Xanthe's silver eyes looking back at him from the page. It's as if he had once again been sent to lead the travelers safely to their next Essence of Wind and Air. Grandpa briefly shared with Finn the name and meaning of his friend, the fox, Xanthe. "He has been sent to us once again, my wise and sly friend from long ago." Mira looked at the map where Xanthe's image had appeared and knew in her heart that her dreams of Xanthe last night were a message meant for her. There was no reason to be anxious; the magic of the Hollow was still with them as they strove to complete their healing quest.

THE ESSENCE OF WIND AND AIR

Soon after discovering the symbol of Xanthe on the Ancient Text, Grandpa and Mira had gathered their belongings, and the group had set out to obtain the Essence of Air and Wind. The fairies were excited to be a part of this group. Along the way, wildflowers were growing everywhere. Lilibelle and Elira stopped along the way to smell them. Pippa began stopping as well. The flowers were irresistible to the female fairies. It's almost like catnip to a cat. While Pippa and everyone else were admiring the beautiful blooms, Niko wandered off with no one realizing it. When they were ready to continue, they saw that Niko was nowhere to be found. Pippa was so upset with herself for taking her attention off her small charge. Grandpa went down one path, the fairies down another, and Mira and Ari went down still another path. They were all calling for Niko. Ominously, there was no answer. They all met back at the clearing in the garden, worried about where he could have slipped off to. There were two more trails to explore. They did it together this time, hoping no one else would wander from the group accidentally.

As they went down the last trail, they heard water running. This caused dread because Niko barely knew how to swim. Ari had just started teaching her little brother at the beginning of the past summer. They all ran frantically toward the water's edge and found Niko playing in the shallow water, finding special rocks for his slingshot. Grandma and Ari ran to him and gave him a big hug. Grandpa scolded him a bit for wandering off. "I just heard the sound of the brook and knew there would be the right kinds of stones for my slingshot. I'm sorry for worrying everyone." Pippa alighted on his small arm and said, "Never scare me like that again, little one!"

Since they were already at the water's edge, Grandpa suggested a respite from the heat of the day. "We should all take our socks and shoes off and soak our feet. Mine are overheated like the rest of me." Soon, everyone was splashing and playing with one another in the brook. Finn was the only one who didn't participate. He took the time to look at the ancient text and maps they were being guided by. On the page adjacent to the silver fox's symbol were some new symbols that hadn't been there earlier that morning when he and Grandpa Bram had looked it over. He took the map and text to Grandpa Bram and showed him his discovery. What could these symbols mean, Finn?" Bram asked.

Finn traced his finger over the first symbol, a delicate crescent moon. "This could represent a hidden location that is only accessible at night or during a specific lunar phase." Then he moved to the second symbol, an eye. "And this eye…it signifies a place of great wisdom or a guardian that watches over a secret." Bram's eyes followed Finn's finger as it moved to a small, intricately drawn owl perched above the eye. "The guardian of the eye is an owl," Finn continued. "Owls are known for their wisdom and keen sight. This must be a place where we can find important knowledge and guidance.

Bram nodded thoughtfully. "We should head there next. The owl might have the answers we need."

THE WISE OWL

As the moon rose high in the sky, casting a silvery glow over the landscape, the group prepared to set out on their journey. The air was cool and filled with the sounds of the night, adding an air of mystery to their quest.

"We should leave now," Finn said, folding the ancient map carefully and tucking it into his satchel. "The owl will guide us to the place of wisdom."

Grandpa Bram nodded, his eyes reflecting the determination of their mission. "Let's find the owl and uncover the secret it guards."

The group moved silently through the forest, their path illuminated by the soft light of the crescent moon. The trees whispered secrets as they passed, and the night creatures watched with curious eyes. After a while, they reached a clearing where an ancient tree stood tall and proud. Perched on one of its branches was a majestic owl, its eyes gleaming with an otherworldly wisdom. Finn stepped forward, holding up the map. "We seek the knowledge you guard, Wise Owl." The owl tilted its head, studying the group with its keen gaze. "To find what you seek, you must prove your worth." His voice echoed through the clearing. "The Essence of Wind and Air and the Essence of Fire are hidden in places where only the brave and the wise can reach."

Bram stepped forward, his voice steady. "We are ready to face any challenge. Tell us where to find the Essences."

The owl nodded. "The Essence of Wind and Air is hidden in the highest peak of the Whispering Mountains, where the winds speak in ancient tongues. The Essence of Fire lies deep within the Heart of the Volcano, guarded by the flames of old."

Finn and Bram exchanged determined glances. "We will find them," Finn said. "Thank you, wise Owl."

The owl spread its wings and took flight, disappearing into the night sky. The group stood in the clearing, their hearts filled with a renewed sense of purpose.

"Let's head to the Whispering Mountains first," Bram suggested. "We need to find the Essence of Wind and Air." With their path set, the family and its fairy friends continued their journey, ready to face the challenges that lay ahead.

THE WHISPERING WINDS IN THE MOUNTAIN TOPS

The group rested for a few hours before attempting to climb the mountain peak. Once rested and refreshed, they headed down the path to the mountain with excitement and determination. They kept a steady pace and found themselves ascending the mountain steadily. The farther they ascended, the harder it was to continue due to fierce winds that carried ancient whispers. They must decipher the whispers to find the correct path, but the winds are strong and disorienting. Ari and Niko held on to Grandma and Grandpa's hands. The fairies were tucked deep into the children's shirts so as not to be blown away. It was Lilibelle and Elira who began making sense of the whispers. They told Ari and Niko so they could tell Bram and Mira, "The winds are saying to beware the bridge of clouds." It's a narrow and invisible bridge made of clouds that we must cross. The bridge is only visible when the moonlight hits it at a certain angle, and we must time our crossing perfectly."

Grandma and Grandpa found an alcove where they could all duck into to find shelter from the fearsome wind. It wasn't a very big alcove, but it was big enough when the children sat on their grandparents' laps. While they were recovering from the crazy windstorm in the little alcove, they kept an eye out for the bridge of clouds. They spoke quietly with one another, still excited about the prospect of finding the Essence of Air and Wind. The fairies began fluttering their wings and going from one person to the other, making sure everyone was okay. The fairies didn't remember such fierce wind in all their lives. Bram and Mira reassured them that they were all fine after double-checking with their grandchildren themselves. As they sat in the alcove, the wind outside seemed to pick up and become even fiercer. While they waited for the wind to die down a little bit, the fairies took turns peeking out at the mountainside to see if the moon was revealing a bridge of clouds yet. When it was Thistle's turn to keep watch, he saw it and shouted to the others. "I see it! The whispers in the wind were right. The bridge of clouds can be seen right now!" The others moved quickly in order to cross over the bridge lit by moonlight. First, Grandpa ventured out and led Grandma Mira and the children toward the bridge. As they climbed even higher than they were, the fairies were able to flit about and come back to them, reporting any dangers they saw ahead. When the way seemed clear, the foursome continued past the bridge of clouds, up the mountainside to the peak. Snow capped the mountain top. Even during summer in the Hollow, snow was visible on the peaks of the surrounding mountain peaks. When they were past the bridge, the wind began whispering again. The fairies heard the word of the wind and interpreted it for the humans. "On the mountaintop, you will find a cave to enter. You can stay there and rest. The guardian of Air and Wind will meet you there."

When they reached the mountaintop, they saw the cave and entered it. It had been a long trek for the weary bunch. They all lay down to rest for a few hours. It would be daylight soon enough. They all slept peacefully, and Grandma Mira was the first to awaken. She began gathering their food from the backpacks and making a nice breakfast for the grands. They all looked to be sleeping peacefully. She decided to let them rest a bit longer as she lay down herself. Grandpa Bram was lightly snoring, a sound she had come to know well. It was so hard to believe they had been married for almost 50 years. She still felt young, and Bram still acted young, still strong and decisive. She lay down beside him and soon drifted off again.

THE GUARDIAN OF WIND AND AIR

It was midmorning when the group began to stir and awaken. Ari and Niko found the food Grandma Mira had set out for them and ate hungrily. That long trek last night had given them quite an appetite. Grandpa Bram and Grandma Mira awoke next. The fairy folk were still sleeping. Ari and Niko were anxious to meet the Guardian the wind had whispered about. Grandpa had the ancient text and maps in front of him. He wanted Finn to wake up and look it over to see if there had been any changes. Ari began waking the fairies. They were majestic-looking this morning, their wings reflecting their peaceful sleep and relaxation. Finn flew over to Bram. He began studying the ancient text and maps with him. As they were looking, a picture of an eagle appeared. "This must be a picture of the Guardian of Wind and Air," Finn said to everyone. Then, at the opening of the cave, a huge eagle came to rest in front of them all. He was a beautiful creature with a golden brown head, sleek like a cat's fur. He thanked them for coming and waiting for him. He had been busy with other matters when he received the message that they were coming for the Key to the Essence of Wind and Air. "I picked the key up for you on my way home." The magnificent creature handed a key to Bram with its talons. It was fancy-looking. Finn admired it in the palm of Grandpa's hand. "I have seen pictures of this key in the past. I never thought I would have the chance to touch it." Thistle, Pippa, Lilibelle, and Elira fluttered their wings and hovered above Grandpa's hand that held the magnificent key. "Thank you so much, Guardian." The fairy folk asked the beautiful bird for instructions on what to do with the key. He said, "You will know when the time comes what to do with the key."

THE JOURNEY DOWN THE MOUNTAIN INTO THE HOLLOW

After the magnificent bird flew away, they began gathering their belongings. Finn and Grandpa furled the map and ancient text, putting them in their backpack. The fairies helped return the cave to its condition before they had to stay there. They sprinkled fairy dust all around, hoping to make it seem cozy for the next guests.

Grandpa led the way down the mountainside. There were so many flowers in bloom, which happened to be the fairies' favorite. As they walked downhill, Grandpa was already thinking about the final Essence they needed to gather. They now needed to gather the Essence of Fire. This is the most dangerous of the elements; its essence would be more challenging than any of the others had been. This worried him just a bit because the group was tired and in need of a break from the stress of pursuing the Essences. While it had been a wonderful adventure thus far, the children were looking rather worn out. Bram suggested to Mira that they make a stop at their cottage and spend at least one night there before striking out in search of the Essence of Fire. After looking at the faces of the children and their fairies, she agreed it was time to reboot.

HOME SWEET HOME

The children and fairies were so happy to see the cottage and its beautiful garden. Adventures were nice, but coming home was one of the best parts. Grandma Mira and Grandpa Bram went to their chairs in the sitting room. It was definitely nice to be home.'

The fairies went out to the garden and curled up in the buttercups, except Thistle and Finn. They were in the library, finding books to read about the essences of earth, wind, fire, and water. They wanted to see if there was information written in the books that could help them along the way to gather the Fire Essence.

Soon enough, the weary travelers turned in for the night and had more dreamscapes.

Morning in the Hollow

The Hollow awoke with a gentle hush, sunlight spilling through the trees in golden ribbons. Dew sparkled on the grass like tiny gems, and the air carried the crisp promise of adventure. Ari shaded her eyes from the brightness of the sun. Beside her, Niko skipped along the path, humming to himself, his excitement bubbling over.

The five fairies gathered in a circle, their wings catching the morning light. Lilibelle glowed softly, like the warmth of the sun itself. Pippa darted ahead of Niko, leaving trails of laughter that mingled with birdsong. Thistle's sharp gaze swept the forest, alert even in the calm. Finn strode forward with bold confidence, his wings flashing like sparks. And Elira—her wings shimmering with an ember-like glow—lingered close, her presence steady and radiant. "This is the day." Elira said, her voice carrying like music through the trees, "The fire waits for those who are brave enough to seek it."

Ari glanced at Niko, radiant. "Are you sure we're ready?" Niko grinned, his eyes wide with wonder. "I've been ready since the sun came up." Their grandparents exchanged a knowing look. "Remember," Grandmother said gently, "fire is not only heat. It is courage, and it is light."

"Treat it with respect, and it will guide you."

With hearts pounding, the family and their fairy companions stepped into the forest. The morning path shimmered faintly, as though lit by unseen sparks, leading them deeper into the Hollow toward the place where fire itself waited to be found.

The morning path led them deeper into the Hollow until the trees parted to reveal a clearing unlike any other they had seen. At its center stood a circle of ancient stones, each one etched with glowing runes that pulsed like embers. Above the altar, at the heart of the circle, hovered a flame—small, steady, and impossibly bright in the daylight.

Elira's wings shimmered with a fiery glow as she stepped forward. "This is the essence of fire," she said softly. "It will not burn your skin, but it will test your hearts. Only those who carry courage within them may touch it.

Ari felt her stomach twist. She was ten now. She was old enough to understand danger and old enough to worry. She glanced at Niko, who was already leaning forward, eyes wide with wonder. "Wait," Ari whispered, catching her brother's sleeve. "We have to be careful."

Thistle nodded approvingly. "Fire respects caution, but it also demands boldness."

Finn grinned. "Then let's see what the two of these are made of!"

Lilibelle floated closer, her glow wrapping Ari in calm. "You don't have to be fearless," she said gently, "you only have to be willing."

Ari took a deep breath and then reached for Niko's hand. Together, they stepped into the circle. The flame flickered, stretching toward them, as if curious. "Ready?" Ari asked, her voice trembling. "Ready," said Niko without hesitation. The flame bent lower, brushing against their joined hands. It was warm, but not painful—a heat that filled their chests with light. Ari felt her fear melt away, replaced by a steady strength. Niko laughed, his eyes shining.

Elira raised a crystal vial, and the flame flowed into it like liquid gold, swirling until it settled into a steady glow. "You have done it," she said. "The essence of fire is yours!"

The stones dimmed, the runes faded, but Ari and Niko carried the glow in their hearts, knowing they had faced the trial together—and knowing they had passed.

JOINING THE ESSENCES

Grandma and Grandpa were proud of Ari and Niko for their courageous spirits, capturing the essence of fire. It was now time to bring the essences together. Grandpa had done some research on the ancient text that referred to a heartstone in the Hollow, a place where all the magic of the Hollow and the essences culminate. The fairies were very familiar with the heartstone and led the way.

The path was unlike any they had taken before. Mossy stones lit up beneath their feet, each step revealing a faint shimmer that guided them forward. Birds hushed their songs as the group passed, and even the wind seemed to pause, carrying only the soft hum of magic.

Lilibelle floated close to Ari, her golden glow steady. "The heartstone lies at the center of all things," she whispered. "It is where the Hollow breathes."

Pippa darted ahead, her laughter echoing through the trees. "Come on, slowpokes! The Hollow's waiting!" Thistle frowned, scanning the shadows. A faint rustle answered his silence, like leaves whispering secrets to one another. He tightened his grip on the lantern, its glow trembling against the Hollow's walls.

From the darkness, two pinpricks of light blinked—eyes, curious and unafraid. Ari stepped closer, heart thudding, while Niko tugged at her sleeve. "Wait," Niko whispered, "it's not danger; it's—someone watching."

The shadows parted, and a small figure emerged, wings glimmering faintly, as though woven from starlight. It was Elira; she stepped out of the shadows. She was carrying the ember of fire cupped in her palms. Her wings shimmered faintly, but her eyes held a storm. She hovered at the edge of the lantern's glow, as though weighing whether Ari and Niko were worthy of what she carried.

Thistle's frown deepened. "She doesn't trust us," he murmured. The ember in Elira's palms pulsed like a heartbeat, flashing flickers of red across the Hollow. Ari felt the warmth reach her face, causing her to feel comforted. Niko, braver than he realized, whispered, "We will prove ourselves. Tell us what we must do."

Elira tilted her head, her voice soft but edged with fire. "The ember cannot be given; it must be earned. Show me your courage in the shadows, where flame is born from fear."

The Hollow seemed to tighten around them, shadows stretching into shapes that tested their resolve. Ari glanced at Thistle, then at Niko, and nodded. Together, they stepped forward, ready to face whatever trial was required.

The ember pulsed in Elira's palms; shadows were stretching, long and restless. Ari and Niko stood ready, but it was their grandparents who steadied the moment.

Grandma Mira moved closer, her voice calm but firm. "Courage isn't only for the young. We've faced storms before, and we'll face this one together. Her words wrapped around the children like a shield, reminding them that bravery could be quiet and enduring.

Grandpa Bram lifted his walking stick, tapping it once against the stone floor. The sound echoed, sharp and grounding, cutting through the Hollow's illusions in the shadows. "Shadows thrive on fear," he said, "but they falter when family stands united."

The fairies glanced at one another—Thistle's frown softened, and even Elira's fiery gaze flickered with respect. The trial was no longer just for Ari and Niko; it was for the whole group, bound by love and memory.

The shadows shifted, reshaping into forms that mirrored each traveler's doubt. Ari saw hesitation, Niko saw loneliness, and the grandparents saw the weight of age and loss. Yet together, they stepped forward, each lending strength to the other, proving that courage isn't a solitary flame but a shared fire.

The five fairies gathered in a circle, each holding their elemental gift: Thistle with the whisper of wind. Lilibelle with the shimmer of water. Finn with the strength of the Earth. Pippa with the glow of light and Elira with the ember of fire.

Ari and Niko stood at the center, their grandparents beside them, hands linked. As the fairies raised their essences, the elements spiraled together—wind feeding flame, water cooling it, earth grounding it, and light binding them all.

The Hollow filled with a radiant hum, and when the glow faded, a single crystal remained: the Heart of Harmony, pulsing with all five powers combined. Elira placed it in Ari's hands.

Their quest was complete. The Hollow was once again in balance.

Heading Home

Once their quest was completed, it was time for the children and the grandparents to head back to their cottage in the Hollow. They felt accomplished and at peace. They had done it! They were a little weary and anxious to get home. The fairies returned to their homes in fairyland. There was balance once again.

Their little cottage welcomed them home, and they had a peaceful night's rest. The next morning, when the children went out to play, Pippa was in the garden, waiting for them.

She told Niko and Ari that they hadn't forgotten about their grandparents' anniversary celebration. She and the other fairies wanted to help make the plans. Ari and Niko were excited to know that their fairy friends still wanted to be a part of their lives and plans.

It was decided, after speaking to them all, that the fairies would be responsible for the venue while Ari and Niko handled the cake.

THE FAIRIES AND THE VENUE

The Hollow shimmered with anticipation as the five fairies gathered in a circle. Their wings flickered like lanterns in the dusk.

"Under the stars," whispered Lilibelle, tracing a pattern in the air that blossomed into glowing constellations. "The sky itself should be their ceiling."

"No, no," countered Finn, stomping his tiny foot. "A meadow of golden blossoms, each one opening as they walk past." "That's romance!"

Elira raised her hand, her voice calm but firm. "We must honor both elegance and warmth. Fifty years is not only about beauty— it's about endurance."

The fairies tested their magic: vines curled into archways, streams hummed with music, and roses bloomed in pairs, twining together as if they had always been meant to be, like Bram and Mira….

A sudden burst of fireflies swarmed the clearing, and the fairies laughed as they chased them back into neat glowing lanterns. At last, they agreed: a garden of roses, each bloom glowing faintly gold, with lanterns strung above like stars. It was a place where love itself seemed to breathe.

THE CHILDREN AND THE CAKE

Meanwhile, Ari and Niko were knee-deep in flour and determination. The kitchen smelled of sugar and berries, though most of it seemed to cling to their clothes. "Five layers," Ari declared, stacking pans on the counter. "One for each decade." Niko frowned, brushing flour from his nose. If we make it too tall, it will collapse. We need strength, not just height." They experimented. Honey for sweetness, berries for resilience, and chocolate for warmth. Each flavor carried meaning. When the oven sputtered and the cake seemed doomed, Ari grabbed Niko's hand. "We can fix this together!"

With teamwork, they saved the cake, pulling the layers out golden and proud. They decorated it with sugar, roses, and a shimmering "50" on top. Then they noticed the faint glow. The fairies had enchanted the ingredients, and the cake now radiated a gentle light, as if love itself had seeped into the layers.

LATER IN THE DAY

The grandparents stepped into the glowing garden, their hands still entwined after 50 years. Lanterns shivered above them, roses bloomed in pairs, and the cake stood proudly at the center.

Mira's eyes filled with tears. "Do you remember our wedding day?" she whispered. "The rain poured so hard we thought no one would come. But you held my hand, and suddenly the storm didn't matter."

Bram chuckled softly, "I remember we danced in puddles, and you laughed so brightly the clouds seemed afraid to stay."

He turned to the children, his voice thick with emotion, "And now, fifty years later, you've given us a celebration more magical than we could have dreamed." Ari stepped forward, cheeks flushed. "We wanted it to be special. Every layer of the cake means something about your love."

Niko added, "And the fairies made the garden glow just for you!"

Mira bent down, cupping Ari's face, "You've given us a memory that will live in our hearts forever." Bram raised his hand toward the fairies. "And you—guardians of wonder—you've reminded us that love is the greatest magic of all."

Music drifted from the enchanted stream, and the grandparents began dancing beneath the lanterns. Their steps were slower now, but their joy was radiant. The children and fairies watched, realizing they had created more than a celebration. This was a legacy of love.

Ari and Niko exchanged looks with one another, proud of the cake they had made. Just then, there was a rustle in the shadows of the Hollow. They both looked and saw a familiar friend. Xanthe, the fox, with his silver eyes, was also watching.

Author's Note to the Reader: Thank you for reading about the adventures of Ari and Niko. Please look for their next adventure with Xanthe, the silver-eyed fox.